Original title:
Spring's Bursting Blossoms

Copyright © 2024 Creative Arts Management OÜ
All rights reserved.

Author: Thor Castlebury
ISBN HARDBACK: 978-9916-85-790-8
ISBN PAPERBACK: 978-9916-85-791-5

Blooming Dreams

In dawn's embrace, the petals rise,
Whispers of hope in the morning skies,
Each bloom a promise, fresh and new,
Painting the world in vibrant hue.

With every breath, the fragrance spreads,
Awakening souls from silent beds,
In gardens where our visions dance,
We find the magic, we take a chance.

The Colorful Revelation

A canvas vast, where colors blend,
A tapestry of life that will not end,
From violet dusk to golden dawn,
The shades of truth are gently drawn.

In every stroke, a story lives,
In vivid hues, the heart forgives,
Unveiling secrets in the light,
A vibrant world emerges bright.

Hidden Life Unearthed

Beneath the soil, where shadows creep,
Life whispers secrets, quiet and deep,
Roots intertwine in a dance of trust,
A hidden realm in the earth's soft crust.

Unseen wonders begin to bloom,
In the depths of silence, pushing through gloom,
Nature's whispers, a gentle guide,
Revealing the life that thrives inside.

Bliss in Full Bloom

Under the sun, where laughter grows,
Joy bursts forth like a radiant rose,
In every petal, a story told,
Of warmth and beauty, timeless and bold.

With hearts wide open, we celebrate,
The blissful moments that we create,
In gardens of love, forever we roam,
Finding our bliss, where we feel at home.

Color's Resurrection on Fresh Grass

Beneath the dawn, the colors rise,
Emerald blades where sunlight lies.
Each drop of dew, a treasure found,
Awakening life from slumber's ground.

The pastel skies in soft embrace,
Paint the world, a vibrant space.
Petals unfurl in morning's light,
Colors reborn, a splendid sight.

Threads of Life in Blooming Fields

In fields where wildflowers dance and sway,
Nature weaves her threads day by day.
Golden hues against the azure sea,
Intertwine with whispers of the breeze.

Every blossom a story told,
In the tapestry of green and gold.
Roots entwined beneath the earth,
Celebrate the cycle of rebirth.

The Infinity of Nature's Bloom

Petals like stars in a boundless sky,
Infinite beauty that catches the eye.
The fragrance of life in the soft spring air,
A reminder of wonders, forever to share.

With every hue, nature spins her art,
Painting the canvas, a beat of the heart.
In the bloom of the moment, we pause and gaze,
Capturing time in an endless maze.

The Harmony of Blossoms and Bees

In gardens alive with soft buzzing sounds,
Where blossoms and bees dance round and round.

A symphony sweet in the calming breeze,
Harmony flows through the petals with ease.

Golden workers in search of delight,
Kissing each bloom in the warm sunlight.
Nature's orchestra, a melody free,
Echoes the bond of blossoms and bees.

Sunlit Petals

In morning's glow, the petals dance,
A tapestry of hues, in perfect chance.
They catch the light, a vibrant blaze,
Whispering secrets of golden days.

With dew-kissed grace, they bow and sway,
As gentle breezes lead the way.
Each blossom tells a tale unspoken,
Of love and life, eternally woven.

Harmony in Color

In fields where colors intertwine,
Like melodies that softly shine.
Each shade a note in nature's scheme,
Creating canvas for a dream.

The violets hum, while daisies chime,
In unison across the clime.
A symphony of beauty, rich and rare,
In harmony, the world laid bare.

The Beauty of Resurgence

From winter's grasp, the earth awakes,
With tender shoots that gently breaks.
Life pulses through the thawing ground,
In silent strength, new hope is found.

As shadows fade and sunbeams gleam,
Resilience whispers, a quiet dream.
Nature's cycle, strong and true,
Embracing change, as all things do.

Hope in Full Bloom

Amidst the chaos, a flower springs,
Unfolding hope on fragile wings.
With petals wide, it greets the sun,
A testament to battles won.

In every garden, dreams take flight,
Each bloom a spark, a beacon bright.
As colors burst and fragrances weave,
The essence of joy, we all believe.

Blooms in the Glow of Dawn

In the hush of morning light, bright petals do
unfold,
Whispers of a fragrant world, secrets yet untold.
Dew-kissed glories sway and dance, embraced by
gentle breeze,
Nature's canvas paints anew, a masterpiece with
ease.

Among the shadows, colors spark, a symphony of
spring,
Each bloom a story waiting there, with joy and
hope it brings.
As sunbeams weave through branches high, the
day begins to sigh,
In the glow of dawn's embrace, our spirits learn
to fly.

Radiance Unfolding

Beneath the sky of azure dreams, where whispers
softly play,
The vibrant hues of life emerge, announcing
brighter days.
Each blossom opens, skies collide, with laughter
in the air,
In the dawn's warm, gentle light, we shed our
daily wear.

Like golden threads that stitch the morn, our
hopes begin to rise,
We breathe in peace, as shadows fade, beneath
the sunlit skies.
Each heartbeat resonates with joy, in nature's
sweet embrace,
Radiance that fills our souls, we find our sacred
space.

Colors of a New Dawn

When night retreats and shadows melt, a palette
rich and rare,
The dawn unveils its colors bright, as hearts begin
to dare.
From blackest nights to vibrant days, the world
begins to stir,
With strokes of gold, and hues of hope, our spirits
start to purr.

Cascades of pinks and purples blend, in skies of
soft pastel,
Promises within each sunrise bloom, in nature's
wondrous spell.
Awake to beauty all around, as life begins to
show,
The colors of a new dawn rise, igniting dreams
that flow.

The Melody of Reawakening

In the symphony of morning light, a melody
emerges clear,
With notes of joy and whispers soft, inviting us to
hear.
The rustle of the leaves above, the songbirds start
to sing,
A chorus of the waking world, as nature smiles in
spring.

Each sound a thread that weaves us close, to
moments pure and bright,
In harmony with every beat, we step into the
light.
The rhythm of our beating hearts, a dance of
sweet rebirth,
The melody of reawakening, resounds throughout
the earth.

Delight in the Garden's Awakening

In the hush of dawn's first light,
The blossoms stretch, in pure delight,
Greens unfurl with the softest grace,
A symphony of life in this sacred space.

Bees dance gently from bloom to bloom,
Fragrant whispers dispel the gloom,
With every petal, the world renews,
Awakening dreams in vibrant hues.

The Palette of Promise Unfolding

Strokes of color kiss the earth,
In gardens rich with tender mirth,
Lilies and daisies in laughter sway,
A testament to the bright new day.

Sunlight pours like molten gold,
Tales of beauty quietly told,
Every blossom, a canvas bright,
Painting hopes in the warm sunlight.

Earth's Joy in Full Flower

The meadow bursts with life anew,
In fragrant blooms of every hue,
Nature's heartbeat strong and clear,
A joyous hymn for all to hear.

Each bud a promise, each stem a song,
Echoing where we all belong,
The earth adorned in beauty's grace,
A testament to love in this vast space.

The Harmony of Ma Nature's Resurgence

In spring's embrace, the world does sing,
As Ma Nature dances on the wing,
Cherished whispers in the blooms,
Resounding hopes through silent rooms.

Rivers ripple with laughter bright,
And every star awakens the night,
In this chorus, life finds its way,
Celebrating love in a grand display.

A Tapestry of Color in the Breeze

Petals dance upon the air, with grace they find
their flight,
In hues of blush and vibrant blue, they weave a
pure delight.
As sunlight spills through branches green, each
shade begins to sing,
Together they compose a song, a tapestry of
spring.

A canvas strewn with nature's brush, where
whispers softly call,
A symphony of colors bright, enchanting one and
all.
The gentle breeze, a playful hand, unfolds each
soft embrace,
In every flutter, art unfolds, a moment filled with
grace.

The Joyful Chorus of Chirping Birds

In morning's light, the birds awake, their songs a
sweet release,
A joyful chorus fills the skies, a symphony of
peace.
With melodies like silver streams, they flit from
bough to bough,
A vibrant hymn of life unfolds, reminding us of
now.

Each note a spark, each chirp a dream, they
weave through golden air,
A celebration of the dawn, a promise bright and
rare.
The world rejoices in their song, as nature's heart
takes flight,
In every chirp, a dance of joy, a serenade of light.

Ephemeral Beauty in the Morning Light

As dawn awakens, shadows flee, the world begins
to glow,
With dew-kissed petals shimmering bright, the
beauty starts to show.
A fleeting glimpse, a moment caught, in nature's
grand embrace,
Ephemeral wonders rise and fall, a soft and tender
grace.

The sun's first rays, a golden brush, paint life's
delicate design,
Each sparkle holds a whispered wish, as time
slips through the vine.
In every breath of morning's calm, a promise to
hold tight,
For beauty lives in fleeting ways, beneath the soft
daylight.

Nature's Canvas Painted Fresh

Beneath the sky of azure deep, where dreams and
visions dance,
Nature spreads her palette wide, inviting us to
glance.
With emerald fields and mountains bold, she
crafts a splendid view,
In every curve and shade of light, a masterpiece
shines through.

The rivers flow like liquid glass, reflecting day's
embrace,
While clouds like whispers paint the air, in a soft
and dreamy lace.
Each moment glows with vibrant life, a wonder to
behold,
A canvas fresh, where stories bloom, in colors
rich and bold.

Blooms That Brush the Sky

In gardens where the sunlight spills,
Petals dance upon the zephyrs' thrills,
Colors woven in a silken thread,
Nature's canvas, where dreams are fed.

Upward reaching, seeking the blue,
Each flower whispers secrets anew,
Together they form a vibrant sea,
A symphony sung by the bumblebee.

With hues that warm the winter's chill,
And fragrances that time cannot still,
The blossoms sway, a gentle sigh,
In a world where hopes and wishes lie.

They spread their arms, a joyful plea,
Embracing skies so wild and free,
For in their beauty, spirits soar,
In blooms that brush the sky, we explore.

Life's Rebirth in Gentle Shades

Beneath the frost, a whisper stirs,
Awakening dreams that spring prefers,
In gentle shades, the earth does wake,
A tapestry that life will make.

Soft greens unfurl, like morning's breath,
Resilience born from winter's death,
The tender shoots arise, they greet,
In every corner, hope is sweet.

Blossoms peek through the melting snow,
With vibrant pulses, life's ebb and flow,
Each bud a promise, each leaf a sign,
Of moments cherished and hearts entwined.

In sunlight's arms, new stories weave,
The past is gone, but we believe,
With every bloom, a song is played,
In life's rebirth, our fears allayed.

The Secrets of Flora's Flourish

In whispered tones, the flowers speak,
Of hidden worlds where wonders peek,
Delicate petals in the breeze,
Share tales of time beneath the trees.

A violet's blush, a daisy's cheer,
In their embrace, the magic's near,
Each stem a story, each leaf a dream,
In nature's language, all things gleam.

From roots that delve in soil's embrace,
To blooms that dance in boundless grace,
The secrets lie in every hue,
A tapestry of life rings true.

In twilight's gentle, golden glow,
The chorus of both high and low,
In flora's flourish, we are found,
As life unfolds, we are spellbound.

Where the Lilies Laugh in Gold

In a pond where reflections play,
Lilies beam in a bright ballet,
Petals open like hands in prayer,
Their laughter dances on the air.

Cascading ripples, a soft embrace,
The sun dips low, a burning grace,
Each lily blooms like a heart so bold,
In waters kissed by the hues of gold.

With secrets held in layers deep,
They sway and shimmer, never sleep,
Beneath the surface, life abounds,
In this realm where joy resounds.

As twilight falls, their whispers rise,
A serenade beneath the skies,
In laughter shared, the day grows old,
In the place where lilies laugh in gold.

Breaths of Fresh Bloom

In the morn, the petals wake,
Soft whispers cradle the air,
Each dewdrop a promise remade,
Nature's brush strokes without a care.

Colors dance in the gentle breeze,
A symphony only the heart knows,
Canvas of life, designed to please,
With every heartbeat, beauty grows.

Fragrant tales upon the ground,
A chorus of joy with each stride,
Nature's secrets, profoundly profound,
In this oasis, dreams abide.

With every breath, the world anew,
The blossoms breathe, the sunlight beams,
In this moment, we're born anew,
In the garden of endless dreams.

Unfolding Beauty

Petals unfold like whispered sighs,
In the hush of the breaking dawn,
Each flower a story, a sweet surprise,
In gardens where hope is reborn.

The sun weaves gold through emerald leaves,
Casting shadows that dance and play,
In this realm where the heart believes,
Every moment beckons to stay.

Butterflies waltz in the soft sunlight,
While gentle breezes hum their tune,
In this world, all worries take flight,
As day melts into the embrace of the moon.

Here, beauty is not just seen,
But felt in the marrow, alive,
An exquisite tale where love has been,
In the symphony of nature, we thrive.

Garden of Dreams

In the twilight where wishes bloom,
A tapestry spun with celestial thread,
Whispers of stardust, banish the gloom,
In the enclave where the heart is led.

The moonlight kisses the tranquil ground,
Each shadow a lover, a secret to keep,
In the garden of dreams, all lost can be found,
As petals unfurl from the arms of sleep.

Echoes of laughter, the songs of the night,
Guide the way through the fragrant maze,
In this haven where everything feels right,
We dance in a rhythm, lost in a daze.

With every bloom, a story unfolds,
Of hope and of wonder, and love's gentle scheme,

In the garden of dreams, where the heart beholds,

The magic that lies just beyond the dream.

Flowers Sing in Chorus

In the meadow where colors blend,
Petals whisper secrets of the wind,
Each blossom sways with the softest song,
Together they dance, where they all belong.

Sunbeams tickle with a gentle grace,
As bees hum lightly in their busy race,
With every note, the flowers proclaim,
Nature's embrace, forever the same.

In violet hues and golden screens,
They share their dreams in silky sheens,
A symphony played by root and stem,
In the heart of the earth, a vibrant gem.

So let us pause, our worries cease,
And join the blooms in their sweet release,
For every flower sings a part,
In the chorus that echoes within the heart.

The Awakening Garden

From slumber deep, the garden wakes,
With every bud, a promise makes,
The sun's first kiss brings forth new life,
As peace replaces winter's strife.

Emerald leaves unfurl with grace,
In the soft light, they find their place,
Each creature stirs, from hush to cheer,
Spring's warm breath draws all near.

Tulips rise like flames ignited,
While daisies dance, brightly delighted,
In the arms of the tender breeze,
Awakening beauty, a soul's release.

And as the dawn breaks wide and bright,
The garden glows in radiant light,
A symphony of color begins,
In every petal, the warmth of sin.

Nature's Bountiful Gift

Harvest whispers in the cool air,
Golden grains wave without a care,
Fruits hang ripe upon the vine,
Nature speaks, her heart divine.

Crystal streams weave through the land,
Carving stories, ever so grand,
Mountains stand in silent might,
Guardians of day, sentinels of night.

From the smallest seed to the tallest tree,
Life unfolds in harmony,
Each moment a treasure, a story to tell,
In this sacred space where wonders dwell.

So let us gather, with grateful hearts,
For nature's gift, a world of arts,
Boundless beauty, a symphony of light,
In every breath, life takes its flight.

Blooms of Possibility

In the cracks of stone, a flower dares,
Reaching for light, despite the stares,
Each petal unfurls, a tale untold,
A testament to dreams bold.

With colors bright, they break through gray,
Reminding the weary, there's always a way,
In gardens of hope, where wishes reside,
Blooms of possibility, forever our guide.

From shadowed paths to skies of blue,
Life finds a way, in shades anew,
For every struggle, a strength we find,
In the heart of the flower, hope intertwined.

So let your dreams take root and grow,
In the soil of courage, let them flow,
For just like flowers, we too can rise,
And paint our world with endless skies.

Petal-Powered Joy

In gardens where the sunbeams play,
Petals dance in bright array,
Colors whisper to the breeze,
A symphony of joy with ease.

Beneath the canopy of green,
Life awakens, pure and keen,
Every bloom a tale to tell,
In nature's heart, we find our spell.

Nature's Flourishing Heart

In the cool embrace of morning dew,
Life unfurls with every hue,
Whispers of the ancient trees,
Nature's heart beats with the breeze.

With every sprout and budding leaf,
A story starts, beyond belief,
Roots entwine in soil so deep,
A promise made, a promise to keep.

An Ode to New Life

From the earth, a spark ignites,
New beginnings shine so bright,
Tiny sprouts push through the ground,
In their hope, the world is found.

Each fragile grasp towards the sky,
A testament as days go by,
With every breath, the spirit thrives,
A melody of vibrant lives.

The Magic of Blossoming

In quiet moments, petals unfold,
Stories written, timeless and bold,
A fragrance whispers dreams untold,
In every bloom, a magic to hold.

The canvas painted by the sun,
Life's tapestry has just begun,
With each new flower, hearts ignite,
The world awakens, pure delight.

The Dance of New Beginnings

In dawn's embrace, where shadows flee,
A canvas waits for dreams to be.
With every step, we shed the past,
The future calls, the die is cast.

Each heartbeat sings a fresh refrain,
Through every joy, through every pain.
With open hearts, we find our way,
A dance of hope, a brand new day.

Whispering Blooms

Among the petals, secrets hide,
In colors bright, their voices glide.
A gentle breeze tells tales of old,
In fragrance sweet, their truth unfolds.

Each blossom speaks in silent grace,
Of sunlit paths and shaded space.
They whisper dreams in muted tones,
In nature's voice, the heart finds homes.

Life's Vibrant Tapestry

Threads of laughter, shadows cast,
Woven stories, futures vast.
In every stitch, a memory sewn,
Life unfolds, the seeds we've grown.

Rich hues of joy, deep shades of strife,
Intertwine in the fabric of life.
With every tangle, beauty springs,
In life's embrace, our spirit sings.

The Garden's Serenade

At twilight's glow, the garden sighs,
As crickets play beneath the skies.
With softest notes, the flowers sway,
In harmony, they weave their play.

The moonlight dances on the leaves,
Where whispers of the night retrieve.
In nature's chorus, peace is found,
A serenade, where dreams abound.

Fragrance in the Air

A whispering breeze through the clover hangs,
Carrying secrets where the wildflower swangs.
Each petal a story, each scent a soft kiss,
Echoes of nature's sweet, hidden bliss.

Dewdrops like diamonds on blades of green,
Dance playfully beneath the sun's golden sheen.
In this fragrant moment, the world feels anew,
A symphony brewed, just for me and you.

Blossoms of Renewal

Beneath the weight of winter's cruel hold,
Hope stirs in silence, a tale to be told.
With each budding leaf, a promise takes flight,
Emerging from shadows, embraced by the light.

Petals unfurl like arms wide with glee,
Welcoming sunlight, as warm as can be.
In gardens of solace, where dreams intertwine,
Life dances again, in colors divine.

Radiant Awakening

As dawn breaks with laughter, the night takes its
leave,
Nature awakens, inviting us to believe.
A tapestry woven with threads of the day,
In radiance kissed, the dark fades away.

The chorus of songbirds, a jubilant choir,
Ignites the horizon, setting hearts afire.
Each moment a treasure, a gift from the sun,
In this radiant awakening, we become one.

A Palette of Rebirth

Brushstrokes of color upon canvas so bright,
Nature's own palette, a mesmerizing sight.
Violet, and gold, with splashes of green,
A vivid reminder of all that's unseen.

Seasons blend softly in an artist's embrace,
Restoring the earth with a delicate grace.
In the hues of revival, our spirits take wing,
A celebration of life, and all that it brings.

Sunbeams and Petals

In the morning light, joy takes flight,
Petals unfurl in radiant delight,
Golden sunbeams weave through the air,
Nature's dance, a beauty so rare.

Whispers of warmth in the softest breeze,
Caressing flowers like tender pleas,
In the meadow, secrets softly share,
A symphony of colors, beyond compare.

The Tapestry of Growth

Threads of time, woven with care,
Sprouts emerge from earth's warm lair,
Every season, a vivid hue,
Nature paints a story anew.

Roots dig deep while branches reach high,
Underneath the vast, embracing sky,
In the silence, whispers of dreams,
A tapestry of life, bursting at the seams.

Flowers' Gentle Embrace

In a garden wrapped in twilight's glow,
Petals fold softly where dreams gently flow,
A hug of colors, a fragrant release,
In every bloom, the heart finds peace.

Beneath the moon's watchful, silver gaze,
Flowers sway softly in a melodious haze,
Each blossom whispering love's sweet tune,
A cradle of beauty beneath the moon.

The Canvas of Color

Brushstrokes of nature, so vibrant, so bold,
A canvas of colors, a story unfolds,
From vibrant reds to softest blues,
Each shade a memory, a moment to choose.

In the garden's heart, artistry blooms,
Creating a world where magic looms,
With every season, a new artwork's grace,
A dazzling display, a warm embrace.

Radiant Rebirth

In dawn's embrace, the shadows flee,
A gentle light sets the world free,
Whispers of flowers in vibrant sway,
Life unfurls in a grand ballet.

The air is laced with sweet perfume,
Nature dances, dispelling gloom,
Each petal soft, each leaf aglow,
A canvas painted in radiant flow.

The Melody of Nature's Awakening

With every chirp, the morning sings,
Awakening the joy that spring brings,
Bees buzz softly, a dulcet tune,
As earth rejoices beneath the moon.

Streams murmur secrets to the trees,
Carrying whispers on a playful breeze,
A symphony crafted, pure and bright,
Nature's awakening, a pure delight.

Garden of Echoes

In the garden where memories dwell,
Echoes of laughter weaves its spell,
Petals fall like whispers from the past,
In every moment, forever cast.

Old trees sway with stories untold,
Guardians of time, both wise and bold,
Roots intertwined beneath the ground,
In this sanctuary, peace is found.

Colors Awakening

The canvas stretches, a vivid show,
From emerald greens to sunset's glow,
Brush strokes of passion fill the air,
A palette bright, beyond compare.

Violet dreams and golden rays,
Nature whispers in colorful praise,
Each hue a heartbeat, a song confined,
Colors awakening, in hearts aligned.

A Floral Celebration

In gardens bright where colors gleam,
Blossoms sway like a painter's dream,
Petals dance in the gentle breeze,
Nature's canvas, a symphony to please.

Butterflies flit from bloom to bloom,
A fragrant waltz that dispels the gloom,
Every flower a story to share,
In this joyful realm, love fills the air.

Soft Whispers of Green

Beneath the boughs where shadows play,
Green whispers settle at end of day,
Mossy carpets invite to rest,
Nature's embrace, a soothing vest.

Leaves rustle softly in twilight's grace,
In their hush, we find a sacred space,
An emerald world where dreams transcend,
In each gentle rustle, our spirits mend.

Emergence of Eden

From the earth, life awakens anew,
Sprouts rise up, kissed by the dew,
Fruits of labor hang low and sweet,
In Eden's heart, our hearts repeat.

Sunlight filters through branches high,
Painting shadows as time drifts by,
Each bloom a testament, vibrant and bold,
In this paradise, stories unfold.

Petals Like Confetti

In the breeze, petals take flight,
A celebration of color, pure delight,
They twirl and tumble, joyous and free,
Nature's confetti for all to see.

With each step, a soft crunch below,
As memories linger where wildflowers grow,
In this moment, we dance and play,
With petals like confetti, our worries allay.

Tender Green Murmurs

In the hush of a morning, soft whispers arise,
Gentle tendrils stretching beneath cobalt skies.
Each leaf holds a secret, each bud a tale,
Wrapped in the warmth where the sunbeams sail.

Nature's lullaby croons to the weary heart,
With tender green murmurs, a delicate art.
The dance of the branches in a sweet embrace,
Invites weary souls to find solace and grace.

Blooms Beneath the Sun

In a garden adorned with fiery hues,
Blooms awaken, shedding the night's dews.
Petals unfurling, like laughter in bloom,
Beneath the bright sun, dispelling the gloom.

With every warm ray, they sway and they spin,
Reflecting the joy that blossoms within.
Colors collide in a vibrant display,
A symphony of life in a radiant array.

Petals in the Breeze

A soft wind brushes past, caressing the flowers,
Petals in the breeze dance through golden hours.
They twirl and they flutter, in playful flight,
A delicate ballet, a pure delight.

With whispers of spring in each gentle sway,
Nature's sweet chorus, a love song at play.
Among the bright blossoms, dreams come alive,
In the heart of the garden, where hopes thrive.

The Joy of Blooming

From silent slumber, the earth starts to wake,
With the joy of blooming, a promise to make.
Each flower a canvas, with stories to share,
Painted by sunlight with tender care.

The fragrance of life fills the air as they rise,
A chorus of colors beneath sunny skies.
In moments of stillness, we pause to behold,
The wondrous beauty of life's tales, untold.

Awakening the Slumbering Garden

In the hush of dawn, whispers take flight,
The petals unfold, kissed by the light,
Every brown stem, a promise reborn,
As life stirs anew from the depths of the morn.

Soft tendrils reach from the soil's embrace,
Dancing with joy in their newfound space,
Rustling leaves chant in a vibrant spree,
The garden awakes, alive and free.

Fragrance of Renewal and Hope

Petals unfurl with a gentle sigh,
A fragrance of sweetness drifts softly by,
Fes ting new songs of resilience and cheer,
Woven through seasons, we hold them dear.

Bright hues emerge from shadows that dwelt,
Each scent a reminder, with courage we felt,
Hope dances lightly on the warm evening breeze,

In the garden of dreams, the spirit finds ease.

Symphony of Life in Full Bloom

Nature orchestrates a melodic spin,
As blossoms burst forth, life's praises begin,
Bees hum a tune, a vibrant refrain,
A symphony woven in sunshine and rain.

Colors collide in a canvas of grace,
Every bloom tells of its beautifully unique place,
Winds carry whispers of tales yet untold,
In the heart of the garden, life dares to be bold.

Tender Buds Beneath the Gentle Rain

Beneath the grey skies, the earth drinks deep,
Tender buds awaken from winter's sleep,
Gentle rain taps like a lover's caress,
Nourishing dreams that the flowers express.

Each droplet a promise, a lover's embrace,
Encouraging growth in this sacred space,
As life stirs beneath the shimmering veil,
A soft symphony sings with the whispering gale.

Dew-Kissed Dreams

In the hush of morn, a whisper glows,
Dew-kissed petals dance on fragile toes.
Each shimmering bead, a fairy's sigh,
Holding the secrets of dreams passing by.

Beneath a canvas of soft, velvety grey,
Hope unfurls softly, like clouds in ballet.
A lullaby plays in the gentle embrace,
Where time flows slowly, in nature's grace.

Nature's Gentle Lullaby

Beneath the arch of the willow's sway,
A melody drifts through the golden hay.
Crickets join in as the twilight descends,
Singing sweet whispers, where silence mends.

The brook murmurs secrets to stones in its path,
As fireflies spark in a rhythmic dance bath.
Nature's soft cradle rocks hearts into dreams,
In the symphony born from the earth's gentle
themes.

Blooms That Breathe

Among the meadows, their colors unfold,
Blooms of affection, stories untold.
Each petal a painter, each hue a song,
In the garden of life, where beauty belongs.

With whispers of pollen on warm summer air,
They sway with the breeze, in a passionate flare.
Reaching for sunlight, their hearts open wide,
In the tender embrace of the world, they confide.

The Softest Hues of Dawn

As night gently bows to the brightening sky,
The softest hues emerge, in a delicate sigh.
Peach and lavender stretch across the expanse,
Awakening dreams in a celestial dance.

With every brushstroke, the day comes alive,
Nature's awakening where wonders survive.
In the tender light, all worries dissolve,
As the promise of morning begins to evolve.

Nectar's Call in the Blossoming Air

In the morning light, where the petals unfold,
A symphony dances, secrets retold.
With whispers of sweetness, the air is imbued,
Nature's own promise, a fragrant prelude.

Bees flit like dancers, their movements divine,
Gathering nectar, a treasure to mine.
Every bloom sways, a soft, gentle sigh,
Inviting the sun, as the day drifts by.

Blossoms That Sing to the Heart

Petals of color, a tapestry bright,
Each hue tells a story, in morning's soft light.
A chorus of whispers, the blooms start to play,
Melodies woven in nature's ballet.

They sway with the rhythm of love's gentle tune,
Calling to dreamers beneath the warm moon.
Fragrances linger like memories sweet,
In gardens where joy and serenity meet.

The Garden's Fanfare of Delight

A burst of vibrant colors, the garden shines,
Lavished in splendor, where joy intertwines.
Each flower a note in this harmonious space,
The world slows its pace, wrapped in nature's
embrace.

Sunlight cascades through the branches above,
Bringing warmth to the blossoms, a symphony of
love.
Their laughter erupts in a gentle cascade,
A fanfare of delight that will never fade.

Whispering Blooms of Diversity

In every corner, a story unfolds,
With blossoms of wonder, their beauty beholds.
Diverse in their natures, yet united in grace,
Whispering secrets, they share their own space.

From the dainty forget-me-nots to tall sunflowers,

Creating a tapestry of vibrant hours.
In this garden of life, all voices are heard,
Celebrating differences with each blooming word.

Soft Blooms Against the Sky

Delicate petals whisper in the breeze,
A dance of colors sways among the trees.
With hues of dawn, they paint the world anew,
Soft blooms against the sky, a vibrant hue.

In gardens tucked where sunlight gently plays,
Nature's secrets bloom through warm, enchanting days.
Each blossom tells a story, bright and bold,
As nature's tapestry begins to unfold.

They catch the eye, a fleeting glance of grace,
A moment's joy in this hectic, hurried race.
Like laughter shared beneath the open air,
Soft blooms against the sky, beyond compare.

As twilight falls, their fragrance lingers still,
A gentle reminder of time's tender will.
In every petal, a heartbeat softly sighs,
In the garden's arms, where hope never dies.

A Haiku of Blossoms

Cherry blossoms sway,
Whispers of spring in the air,
Petals kiss the breeze.

Nature's soft embrace,
A canvas of murmured dreams,
Life blooms with each breath.

Quiet moments pass,
Underneath the azure sky,
Blossoms tell their tale.

The Quiet Symphony of Flowers

In the still of dawn, where shadows softly creep,
The flowers awaken from their gentle sleep.
Their colors weave a harmony so rich,
A quiet symphony, nature's perfect pitch.

Daisies nod in unison, a joyful dance,
While roses blush with love in every glance.
Each petal strums a note on morning's stage,
An ode to life, unfurling page by page.

Lavender hums a tranquil melody,
While lilies sway with noble majesty.
Together they compose a fragrant tune,
A symphony played beneath the silver moon.

As day gives way to dusk, their song remains,
In twilight's hand, an echo still sustains.
In quiet gardens where the heart takes flight,
The flowers sing their secrets through the night.

Life Unfurling

In the cradle of soil, a seedling takes form,
Through struggles and darkness, it braves every storm.
With gentle persistence, it stretches for light,
Life unfurling its arms, reaching wide and bright.

Each leaf a testament to the trials faced,
Each blossom a miracle, beautifully graced.
As roots intertwine in a dance so profound,
Life unfurling beneath the hard, sacred ground.

From whispered beginnings to glorious height,
Nature's promise unfolds, a breathtaking sight.
In the embrace of the sun, the rain's sweet kiss,
Life unfurling blossoms into endless bliss.

In every season, a cycle renewed,
With courage and hope, destiny pursued.
From the tiniest sprout to the tallest tall tree,
Life unfurling sings of what's meant to be.

Petal-Powered Joyride

In the garden where the blossoms sway,
Petals dance like whispers in the day,
Colors burst in a jubilant spree,
A carnival of hues, wild and free.

Dragonflies flit with wings aglow,
Chasing joy in a spiraling show,
With each bloom that opens wide,
Life's bright laughter, a sweet joyride.

Breezes carry the scent of delight,
As sunbeams paint each moment bright,
Together they sing in harmonious cheer,
A symphony of nature drawing near.

So let us wander where petals lead,
Embracing the joyous, unfettered creed,
For in every color, every bloom's sigh,
Lies the heartbeat of a vibrant sky.

Nature's Kaleidoscope

Through the forest, colors blend and twist,
An artist's palette, nature can't resist,
Emerald leaves, and golden light,
In this canvas, tranquility ignites.

Rivers glimmer like sapphire gems,
Dance of shadows, where sunlight stems,
Each creature a brushstroke, vivid and rare,
Painting stories in the crisp, fresh air.

Mountains rise, draped in a tapestry wide,
Soft twilight whispers, where dreams reside,
In every corner, beauty unfolds,
Nature's kaleidoscope, a wonder to behold.

As seasons change, the colors shift,
A reminder to see life's boundless gift,
In the glow of dawn, the hush of night,
Nature's masterpiece, forever in sight.

A New Chapter of Color

With the dawn comes a brush dipped in gold,
Awakening the world as stories are told,
Each petal unfurls with secrets to share,
In this vibrant tale, all hearts lay bare.

A canvas spread wide beneath azure skies,
Fingers of sunlight where every dream lies,
Through valleys and hills, colors ignite,
A new chapter unfolds in the soft morning light.

Roses, violets, and lilacs cascade,
In every hue, memories are made,
With laughter and love threaded through time,
A song of colors, a joyous rhyme.

So paint your life with bold strokes and grace,
Embrace every moment, every place,
With a heart full of wonder, let colors flow,
In this endless journey, let your true self glow.

The Enthralled Earth

Beneath the azure, the earth spins so bright,
Enthralling all with its natural light,
Mountains stand proud, and valleys rejoice,
Nature whispers softly, a lover's voice.

Each rhythm of life, a ceaseless dance,
In the rustling leaves, the sweetest romance,
From oceans that roar to the stars above,
The earth holds our secrets, our dreams, and our
love.

With every sunrise, new wonders ignite,
Painting the canvas with day and with night,
In the pulse of the soil, in the breeze that sways,
Awaits the enchantment of countless days.

So listen closely, for nature's a song,
Where every heartbeat joins the throng,
In this enthralled earth, where beauty begins,
Together we dance, through losses and wins.

Vibrant Veils of Nature

In emerald forests, whispers weave,
Beneath the canopy, the heart believes,
Colors dance in sunlight's embrace,
Nature's palette, a wondrous chase.

Rivers sing with laughter clear,
Mountains stand, majestic and near,
Fluttering leaves, a waltz in the breeze,
Vibrant veils, nature's sweet tease.

Flowers burst in joyous hues,
A canvas bright where life renews,
Every petal, a story to tell,
In nature's realm, we find our spell.

Beneath the skies, where dreams take flight,
Every shade, a song of delight,
With open hearts, we must explore,
Vibrant veils, forevermore.

The Cycle of Bloom

From the barren earth in winter's sigh,
Awakens life as seasons fly,
A tender shoot breaks through the frost,
In the cycle of bloom, nothing is lost.

Petals unfurl beneath the sun,
A symphony played, life's dance begun,
Colors burst forth, a vibrant spree,
In each blossom, a story set free.

Buzzing bees in a joyous race,
Gather the gifts of nature's grace,
In the quiet woods, the fragrance swirls,
The cycle of life, a tapestry unfurls.

When summer fades and leaves turn gold,
The whisper of change begins to unfold,
Yet in decay, there's beauty anew,
The cycle of bloom, eternal and true.

Dappled Light on Petal

Morning breaks with golden hues,
Soft winds carry the sweetest muse,
Dappled light through the canopy spills,
Kissing petals on gentle hills.

Lilies stretch toward the open sky,
While shadows dance as clouds drift by,
In the warmth, colors burst and swell,
A moment captured, a vibrant spell.

As sunlight filters through the trees,
Nature whispers on the breeze,
Each petal glows, a radiant sight,
In the garden's heart, pure delight.

In this sanctuary, peace abounds,
With every heartbeat, beauty surrounds,
Dappled light, a painter's touch,
In nature's arms, we find so much.

Green Reveries

In the hush of the forest's embrace,
Where emerald dreams find their place,
Whispers of leaves in a gentle sway,
Green reveries beckon, calling to play.

Moss carpets the earth, a soft bed,
Through pathways where silent thoughts tread,
Nature's hymn, sung in vibrant tones,
Echoing secrets in sylvan groans.

When sunlight dapples the glade, so fair,
Butterflies flutter without a care,
In every nook, a story unfolds,
Rich with the magic that nature holds.

Lose yourself in the verdant expanse,
Where life's symphony captures a glance,
In the heart of green, let your soul run free,
In deep reveries, just you and the trees.

Cherished Moments in Bloom

In gardens where the sun does gleam,
Petals open, whispering dreams,
A tapestry of colors bright,
Each blossom holds a fleeting light.

The winds caress the fragrant air,
As laughter twirls in nature's care,
Each moment cherished, sweetly sown,
In memories where love has grown.

Beneath the boughs, we sit and sigh,
While butterflies in joys abide,
With every glance, our hearts entwined,
In blooms of spring, true bliss we find.

Together we embrace the dance,
Each glance, a precious second's chance,
In every petal, time stands still,
Cherished moments, hearts to fill.

A Symphony of Fresh Growth

In the silence of the dawn's embrace,
Life awakens, a gentle grace,
Bursts of green in the warm sunlight,
A symphony begins, pure delight.

Roots entwine in the fertile ground,
Whispers of nature's heart abound,
With every sprout, a song takes flight,
In harmony with day and night.

The rustle of leaves, a tender sound,
As creatures stir from underground,
A world reborn, with hope bestowed,
In every heart, fresh dreams are sowed.

Together we celebrate the bloom,
In every corner, life finds room,
A symphony of growth so bold,
A tapestry of stories told.

Echoes of the Earth

In valleys deep and mountains high,
The whispers of the earth comply,
Baby streams sing, a gentle flow,
While ancient trees in silence grow.

Beneath the stars, the stories weave,
Of every heart that dared believe,
With echoes soft as winter's sigh,
And memories of days gone by.

From rocky cliffs to ocean's shore,
The earth resounds, forevermore,
In every grain, a tale does lie,
An archive vast, where dreams can fly.

As twilight falls, the shadows blend,
Each echo speaks of time to mend,
In nature's voice, we find our worth,
Reverberating, the song of earth.

The Canvas of the Seasons

Upon the canvas broad and wide,
Each season paints with joy and pride,
Winter's hush in soft white grace,
Spring's blossoms, a vibrant embrace.

Summer's laughter fills the air,
Golden hues with warmth to share,
Autumn's brush, a fiery glow,
Crimson, amber, nature's show.

Each stroke adds depth to life's design,
In every moment, colors intertwine,
A masterpiece of change and flow,
In the heart of all, the seasons grow.

With every cycle, a tale unfolds,
In whispers of nature, life beholds,
A canvas painted, rich and rare,
In the art of seasons, stories share.

Whispers of the Awakening Earth

Beneath a canopy of morning light,
The earth stirs softly from its slumbered night,
Gentle breezes carry secrets profound,
Whispers of life in the quiet abound.

Roots awaken in the warming ground,
Eyes of nature open, sights unbound,
Emerald leaves dance with stories to tell,
In the cradle of dawn, where magic does dwell.

Birdsong ripples through the crystalline air,
Each note a promise, a shimmering prayer,
Awakening hearts and sowing delight,
In the embrace of the morning's soft light.

The world, reborn from the night's gentle grasp,
Rises anew, in nature's tender clasp,
A symphony of colors, alive and free,
In the whispers of earth, we find unity.

Petals Unfurling in the Sunlight

In the garden's cradle, colors collide,
Petals unfurl, like dreams set aside,
With each gentle touch of the sun's loving kiss,
The world awakens, wrapped in its bliss.

Fragile blossoms dance to the wind's sweet
refrain,
Revealing the secrets of joy and of pain,
Soft hues of lavender and vibrant marigold,
Whispering tales of the brave and the bold.

As shadows retreat and horizons expand,
The language of flowers speaks soft and grand,
Each petal a promise, each fragrance a song,
In the tapestry of life where we all belong.

So let us embrace this fleeting delight,
As petals unfurl in the morning light,
Celebrate the beauty that nature bestows,
In the dance of the blossoms, our spirit grows.

The Dance of Dappled Bloom

In the forest's heart, where shadows play,
Dappled light weaves dreams in a magical way,
Flowers emerge through the whispering trees,
A choreography swaying in the gentle breeze.

A ballet of petals in hues bright and pure,
Each movement a secret, a silent allure,
Nature's performers, stunning and free,
With every soft sway, they beckon to me.

The rhythm of life pulses deep in the soil,
A tapestry woven without any toil,
Underneath canopies, love's sweet embrace,
Nature unfolds in delicate grace.

So let us waltz in this dappled delight,
Come join the dance as day winks to night,
In the beauty of bloom, let our spirits soar,
Together we celebrate, forever wanting more.

Nature's Palette in Vibrant Hues

With a brush dipped in the essence of life,
Nature paints canvas amid joy and strife,
Each hue a story, each shade a refrain,
An explosion of colors, a tempest of rain.

Crimson sunsets bleed into cobalt skies,
Emerald valleys cradle where harmony lies,
Golden meadows sway, kissed by the breeze,
A masterful mural that longs to please.

Lavender whispers stir in twilight's grasp,
And silvery moonlight whispers secrets to clasp,
Nature's expressions, a vivid embrace,
In the heart of each color, life's sweetest grace.

So let us marvel at this vast gallery,
Each stroke a reminder of earth's wonderful story,

In this palette of wonder, let love guide our view,

For in nature's artwork, we find something true.

Blooms as Allusions to New Beginnings

In gardens where the daffodils bow,
Fresh colors awaken from their slumber,
Each petal whispers secrets of the yow,
A promise of tomorrow, hidden wonder.

The lilacs sigh with lilting, soft delight,
Resilient dreams unfurl beneath the sun,
They dance in fragrant breezes, pure and bright,
A tapestry of hope, just begun.

A fragile sprout emerges from the dark,
With every gentle rain, it lifts its head,
Embracing warmth, igniting its own spark,
And finds the strength in paths where few have
tread.

So let us learn from blooms that grace the ground,

In every ending lies a vibrant start,
Their beauty calls us forth, our lives unbound,
New beginnings bloom with whispers of the
heart.

A Sonnet of Life Sprouting Anew

Upon the earth, where winter's breath had laid,
The seeds of life await the sun's warm kiss,
Emerald shoots burst forth, unafraid,
Transcending frost, they rise with hopeful bliss.

With every raindrop's touch, the world awakes,
A symphony of colors starts to play,
In nature's hands, the old foundation breaks,
And fragile blooms unfold to greet the day.

Petals unfurl like stories yet untold,
In their soft grace, the vibrant echoes sing,
The beauty of the earth, in each behold,
Life's cycle turning, ever blossoming.

So let your heart embrace the change it seeks,
For within every season, joy peaks.

Awakening Petals

Awakened from their slumber deep and long,
Petals reach out, a soft and tender touch,
In morning light, they chant a silent song,
Of growth and hope, revealing nature's clutch.

Each bloom a promise wrapped in hues divine,
From vibrant reds to delicate white lace,
With every whispered breeze, they intertwine,
In fragrant appreciation, they embrace.

From tightly closed to blossoming unchained,
They stretch and sway, a dance of time and grace,

In every leaf, a tale of life retained,
Awakening petals, the world they'll face.

Let us, like flowers, embrace our own change,
For in each season, we too can rearrange.

Nature's Color Symphony

In valleys deep where wildflowers bloom bright,
Nature composes her vivid ballet,
A symphony of colors, pure delight,
As petals pirouette in the light of day.

Amidst the greens, the yellows sing aloud,
With blues and violets swirling in the breeze,
A vibrant brushstroke, the earth's tender shroud,
Caressing hearts like soft, melodic keys.

The daisies sway in laughter, free and bold,
While sunflowers gaze at skies of endless hue,
Each note in harmony, a tale retold,
A canvas of existence, fresh and new.

Let us rejoice in nature's grand design,
As colors dance, our spirits intertwine.

Milton Keynes UK
Ingram Content Group UK Ltd.
UKHW020049181024
449757UK00011B/575